MOVING TO PORTUGAL IN 2025

Learn How to Begin a New Life in a Different Country

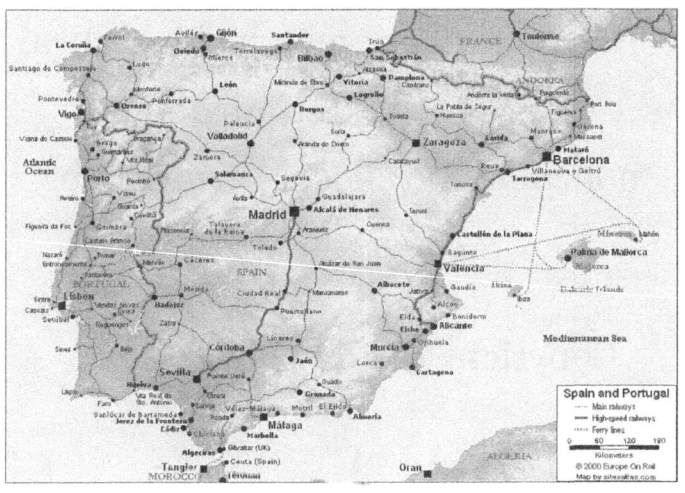

Disclaimer:

The content presented in this Travel guide is derived from the author's research and firsthand experiences, Images are all in black and white.

Although every attempt has been made to ensure the accuracy and thoroughness of the information provided, neither the publisher nor the author can be held liable for any errors, omissions, or changes that may occur subsequently.

Travelers are encouraged to verify the details and make their own arrangements before embarking on any travel plans.

THANK YOU FOR PURCHASING THIS BOOK TO EXPERIENCE PORTUGAL

TABLE OF CONTENT

8

CHAPTER 8

Accommodations

CHAPTER 9

Itineraries

CHAPTER 10

Portugal's Political and Social Landscape

CHAPTER 11

Who This Is For:

This guide is perfect for travelers who want to
experience Portugal in-depth—whether you're a first-time visitor or someone who has seen the Belem Tower and is eager to explore beyond the tourist trail. It's for anyone seeking a more immersive experience, those who want to connect with local culture, and travelers who appreciate uncovering hidden gems.

What Does It Solve:

It solves the problem of incomplete or outdated
information found in a typical Travel guide . By offering insider tips, comprehensive itineraries, and detailed recommendations, this guide eliminates the overwhelm of planning your trip and ensures that you don't miss out on any essential experiences.

What Results Comes From It:

You'll gain a deeper appreciation for Portugal, moving beyond the surface-level tourist attractions and discovering a side of Portugal that many visitors never see. By following this guide, you'll leave with richer memories, stories of hidden places, and the satisfaction of knowing Portugal like a local

Introduction

Portugal. Just saying the name brings a wave of warmth over me, a mix of salty ocean air, the aroma of freshly baked pastéis de nata, and the distant echoes of Fado music in the winding alleyways. This small but incredibly diverse country captured my heart from the first moment I stepped foot here, and if you're considering making the move, I can assure you, you're in for an adventure that will redefine what you call "home."

I've spent a fair share of my time exploring every nook and cranny of Portugal, from its sun-soaked beaches in the Algarve to the lush vineyards of the

Douro Valley, from the bustling, tile-covered streets of Lisbon to the tranquil forests of Serra da Estrela. I didn't just visit Portugal; I lived it. I stumbled through the Portuguese language with friendly locals who never lost their patience, learned to navigate its winding bureaucracy with a smile, and discovered that "saudade" is not just a word but a feeling that becomes a part of you here.

When I first started planning my move to Portugal, I was overwhelmed. The dreamy Instagram photos and travel guides didn't quite prepare me for the reality of organizing my life around a new country. There were visa applications to figure out, cultural nuances to understand, and the monumental task of deciding where to settle down. Would it be the sophisticated charm of Porto, the laid-back vibes of the Algarve, or maybe somewhere lesser-known, like the Alentejo region, where life moves at a slower pace?

But let me tell you: every challenge, every moment of uncertainty, was worth it. Portugal is more than a location; it's an experience that shapes your everyday living. The mornings are slow and intentional, often starting with a café and a pastel de nata at a neighborhood bakery. Afternoons stretch into long, languid lunches, where you might lose track of time over a plate of bacalhau or a hearty bowl of caldo verde. Evenings invite you to wander, to explore cobblestone streets glowing under the lamplight or to sit by the sea, watching the sun dip below the horizon in a blaze of colors that defy description.

By the time 2025 rolls around, Portugal will be more ready than ever to welcome newcomers. The government continues to refine its visa and residency programs, making it easier for expats to settle here. The cost of living remains incredibly attractive compared to other Western European nations, especially for retirees and remote workers. And while cities like Lisbon and Porto are buzzing with activity, there's still plenty of untouched charm to be found in the countryside and coastal towns.

What sets Portugal apart, though, is its people. The Portuguese have an uncanny way of making you feel like you belong. They might tease you for your less-than-perfect pronunciation of "obrigado," but they'll do it with a warmth that feels like an invitation rather than a critique. Their pride in their heritage is palpable, whether they're telling you about their grandmother's secret recipe for arroz de marisco or guiding you to a hidden beach only locals know about.

This book serves as more than a guide—it's your trusted partner every step of the way. I've packed it full of all the things I wish someone had told me when I was planning my move. From practical tips on navigating visas and housing to personal stories about adjusting to life in Portugal, I've made sure there's something here for everyone—whether you're dreaming of a seaside villa, a bustling city apartment, or a quiet home in the countryside.

Moving to Portugal isn't just about relocating; it's about reimagining your life. It's about savoring the moment, appreciating life's simplicity, and discovering beauty in the ordinary. It's about standing on the cliffs of Cabo da Roca, feeling the wind whip through your hair, and realizing that you're exactly where you're meant to be.

CHAPTER 1

Introduction to Portugal

1.1 Overview of Portugal's Culture and History

When I think of Portugal, the first thing that comes to mind is how deeply its culture is intertwined with its history.

Portugal is a country that wears its past proudly—where every cobblestone, tile, and castle tells a story. The Portuguese were once great explorers, charting unknown seas, discovering new lands, and influencing global trade. You feel that legacy everywhere, from the Monument to the Discoveries in Lisbon to the coastal city of Lagos, where Henry the Navigator began his maritime expeditions.

But there's more to Portugal than just its golden age of exploration. This is a land where heritage thrives and roots run strong. The haunting melodies of Fado music capture both sorrow and joy with a rawness that I've never experienced elsewhere. I remember sitting in a dimly lit Tasca in Alfama, a historic neighborhood in Lisbon, as the singer's voice reverberated through the walls. It wasn't just music—it was emotion personified, a connection to the soul of the country.

Portugal's culture also reflects its slower pace of life, which I absolutely fell in love with. There's a focus on savoring moments, whether it's lingering over a morning espresso or sharing a meal with friends and family that stretches late into the night. The people are warm and genuine, always eager to share stories, food, and a little advice for foreigners trying to navigate their home.

Portugal's geography is as diverse as it is stunning. I've driven through the dramatic cliffs of the Algarve, wandered the rolling plains of the Alentejo, and hiked the rugged terrain of the Peneda-Gerês National Park in the north. This country has it all—golden beaches, lush forests, and even snow-capped peaks in winter.

The coastline alone is a marvel. From the iconic beaches of Praia da Marinha to the wind-swept cliffs of Cabo da Roca, there's no shortage of breathtaking views. I spent an unforgettable afternoon walking along the beaches of Nazaré, famous for its monstrous waves that attract surfers from all over the world. The power of the ocean there is humbling, to say the least.

When it comes to climate, Portugal is a dream. The south, especially the Algarve, enjoys more than 300 days of sunshine annually. Summers are warm and dry, perfect for beach days and exploring coastal towns. Winters, while cooler, are still mild compared to other parts of Europe, especially in the southern regions. The north, however, has a different character. Places like Porto and the Douro Valley experience more rainfall, which gives the landscape its lush, green beauty. It's perfect if you enjoy crisp, cool air and cozy evenings by the fire with a glass of local wine.

If you're considering a move to Portugal in 2025, you couldn't pick a better time. The country has been steadily improving its infrastructure for expats, with streamlined visa processes and attractive incentives for remote workers, retirees, and investors.

One of the most appealing aspects for me was the cost-effectiveness. Even with rising tourism, the cost of living remains manageable, especially if you venture outside major cities like Lisbon and Porto. Housing, dining, and healthcare are reasonably priced compared to other Western European countries. I was amazed at how far my euros stretched in smaller towns like Tavira or Guimarães, where life felt both luxurious and accessible.

Portugal also offers a sense of security. It's one of the safest countries in the world, and as a solo traveler and prospective expat, that peace of mind is priceless. Add to that the healthcare system, which is both high-quality and affordable, and it's no wonder so many people are making the move.

But for me, the heart of Portugal's appeal lies in its lifestyle. It's not only about choosing a place to reside; it's about shaping the way you experience life. There's a balance here—a harmony between work, play, and relaxation. It's a place where you can focus on your well-being, whether that means walking along a quiet beach, enjoying a leisurely meal, or simply taking in the stunning landscapes that surround you.

1.4 Key Regions: North, Central, South, and Islands

Portugal is more than just a single destination; it's a tapestry of regions, each with its own character and charm.

North

The north feels like stepping back in time. Porto, the region's crown jewel, is a city that marries the old and the new. The historic Ribeira district, with its narrow streets and colorful facades, feels almost untouched by time. Walking across the Dom Luís I Bridge and savoring Port wine in the cellars of Vila Nova de Gaia is an experience I'll hold dear. Just beyond Porto, the Douro Valley unfolds as a haven for wine enthusiasts. I spent an entire day meandering through its vineyards, tasting wines while overlooking terraced hills that seemed to stretch endlessly into the horizon.

Central

Central Portugal is a region of contrasts. Coimbra, home to a renowned university, is a blend of rich history and vibrant youthful energy. It's also where I witnessed one of the most moving Fado performances, a style unique to this area. The medieval town of Óbidos, surrounded by ancient walls, feels like stepping into a storybook. Then there's Tomar, home to the Convent of Christ, a UNESCO World Heritage Site and a marvel of Templar architecture.

South

The south is all about sunshine and relaxation. The Algarve, with its golden beaches and hidden coves, is one of the most beautiful places I've ever been. I spent a week in Lagos, exploring sea caves and lounging on sandy shores, and another in Albufeira, where the nightlife buzzes with energy. The Alentejo region, often overlooked, is equally captivating. Its endless fields of cork trees and sleepy villages exude a tranquil charm that's hard to resist.

Islands

The Azores and Madeira are Portugal's hidden gems. The Azores, with their volcanic landscapes and thermal springs, are a hiker's dream. I still remember the view from Sete Cidades, a pair of twin crater lakes in striking shades of blue and green. Madeira, on the other hand, feels like an eternal spring. The island's levada walks, winding through lush vegetation and offering panoramic views, are unlike anything else in the world.

CHAPTER 2

Preparing for the Move

When I first decided to move to Portugal, I had no idea what I was truly getting into. Sure, I had heard about the breathtaking landscapes, the world-class food, and the easy going lifestyle, but I quickly learned there's so much more to it. Transitioning to life in Portugal isn't just about booking a flight and packing your bags. It's a process that involves some serious preparation, from understanding visa requirements to adjusting to a new culture and language. Here's a guide to what you can expect when preparing to make Portugal your new home.

2.1 Understanding Visa Requirements

The first thing that hit me was the importance of sorting out my visa situation. Portugal is part of the European Union (EU), but that doesn't mean everyone can come and go freely. The visa requirements differ depending on your nationality, and it's crucial to understand what type of visa suits your situation.

For citizens of the EU, things are straightforward – you don't need a visa to live and work in Portugal. However, if you're from outside the EU, like I was, you'll need to apply for a residence visa. There are several types depending on the purpose of your stay: work visas, student visas, and even special visas for entrepreneurs or retirees. The D7 Visa, for example, is popular for those of us with passive income or pensions, while the Golden Visa allows for investment in Portugal.

One thing I didn't anticipate was how long the process would take. Even though the application process might seem simple, I quickly realized it's a bureaucratic journey, requiring a lot of paperwork. You'll need to provide proof of income, accommodation, health insurance, and sometimes even criminal background checks. While it might feel overwhelming at first, getting all your documents in order ahead of time can save you a lot of stress.

If you're planning to stay for more than 90 days, make sure to look into your specific visa requirements well in advance and allow yourself time for the application process. Trust me, the last thing you want is to be caught up in an unexpected delay.

2.2 Gathering Essential Documents

Once I understood the visa process, I realized just how many documents I would need to gather. It felt like a never-ending list. But each piece of paperwork is a vital part of establishing yourself in Portugal. You'll need your passport, of course, and I also had to get things like proof of income, proof of accommodation, and even a translated copy of my birth certificate.

I made a checklist for myself, so I didn't miss anything. Here's an overview of the essential documents you'll need:

- *Passport* – A valid passport is a must.
- *Proof of Accommodation* – This could be a lease agreement or a hotel booking. I chose to rent an apartment before I arrived, which meant providing a signed contract with the landlord.
- *Proof of Income* – If you're applying for a visa like the D7, they will ask you to

show proof of income or savings, often from a pension or passive income.

- *Health Insurance* – Portugal requires proof of health insurance that covers you during your time there. You can get private health insurance, or if you're an EU citizen, you can use the European Health Insurance Card (EHIC).

- *Background Check* – You may also need a police clearance certificate from your home country, depending on the type of visa you're applying for.

The more prepared you are, the smoother this part of the process will go. My advice is to be patient – some documents may need to be translated or certified, so give yourself plenty of time to gather everything you'll need. I found that making copies of everything and having a file with all the originals helped keep things organized.

2.3 *Researching Cost of Living*

One of the biggest surprises for me, when I started my preparations, was how affordable life in Portugal could be compared to other European countries. Of course, it varies depending on where you live, but in general, Portugal is known for having a lower cost of living compared to places like France or the UK. But even though it's cheaper, it's still important to know what to expect in terms of everyday expenses.

In Lisbon and Porto, the two largest cities, the cost of living is higher than in smaller towns or rural areas. However, even in the capital, rent is still more affordable than other European cities. I was surprised by how much more space I got for my money, especially when it came to renting apartments. Utilities like electricity, water, and internet were also reasonable, though it's important to shop around for the best deals.

One area that I had to adjust to was food prices. While Portugal is known for its delicious food and world-class wine, I found that dining out is incredibly affordable compared to what I was used to in other countries. I could enjoy a fantastic meal at a small restaurant for a fraction of what I'd pay in other cities. If you're a fan of fresh produce and seafood, you'll enjoy the affordability of grocery shopping here, too.

If you're planning to move to the countryside or a smaller town, you'll find the cost of living even lower. I spent some time in towns like Évora and Coimbra, and there, rent and grocery bills were even more affordable. But keep in mind that some of these places, though charming and tranquil, might not have as many job opportunities as the larger cities.

2.4 *Health Insurance and Medical Facilities*

Navigating the healthcare system in a new country can be intimidating, but Portugal has an excellent reputation when it comes to medical care. As an expat, you'll need to make sure you have health insurance. For EU citizens, using the European Health Insurance Card (EHIC) can provide coverage for emergencies, but for non-EU citizens like myself, it's essential to get private health insurance that covers you for the full range of services.

Portugal has a universal healthcare system, the Serviço Nacional de Saúde (SNS), which is highly rated. The public system is affordable and provides access to doctors, specialists, and hospital services. I found that the wait times for non-emergency treatments could be a bit longer than what I was used to, but when I needed urgent care, the service was prompt and efficient.

For more immediate or specialized care, many expats opt for private health insurance. Private healthcare can be more expensive, but it offers quicker access to specialists and a more streamlined experience. I signed up for a private health insurance plan that covered everything from routine doctor visits to dental care, and I've been happy with the service so far.

The great thing about Portugal is that healthcare is top-notch, and there are plenty of well-equipped hospitals and medical centers in cities and towns. I've visited several clinics in Lisbon and Porto, and I've always been impressed by the professionalism and care I've received. Whether you're dealing with a small cold or something more serious, Portugal's healthcare system is there for you.

2.5 *Language and Cultural Adjustment Tips*

Of all the preparations I made before moving, I found adjusting to the language and culture to be the most rewarding part of my journey. The Portuguese language, with its lilting rhythms and distinct sounds, felt like a beautiful challenge. While many people in Portugal speak English, especially in larger cities and tourist areas, learning the local language opened up so many doors for me, both personally and professionally.

I enrolled in a language course before I arrived, which helped me get a solid grasp of basic phrases and vocabulary. Once I arrived, I made it a point to practice speaking with locals whenever I could. The Portuguese are incredibly patient with non-native speakers, and I found that even if my Portuguese wasn't perfect, they appreciated the effort.

Beyond the language, the cultural shift can take a little bit of time. Portuguese people are known for their warmth, hospitality, and strong sense of community. The pace of life is slower than I was used to, which took some getting used to at first, but I soon learned to embrace it. Long lunches, leisurely conversations, and time spent enjoying the company of others are an integral part of Portuguese culture.

I also had to get used to some of the social customs, like the late dinners and the importance of family gatherings. The social calendar revolves around gatherings over food, so being invited to someone's home for a meal is a common and treasured experience. Once I adapted to this slower, more social way of life, I began to appreciate it more than I ever expected.

CHAPTER 3

Finding a Place to Live

Moving to a new country is always an adventure, but one of the most exciting aspects is finding a place to call home. Portugal, with its diverse cities, charming towns, and picturesque countryside, offers a wide range of living options. Whether you're drawn to the bustling city life or the peaceful tranquility of a village, you'll find something that fits your lifestyle.

3.1 *Popular Cities for Expats*

The most popular destinations for expats in Portugal are Lisbon, Porto, and the Algarve region. Lisbon, the country's capital, is a city of contrasts. Its narrow streets in Alfama, alongside grand boulevards like Avenida da Liberdade, give it a charm that's hard to resist. As the cultural and financial hub, Lisbon has a modern cosmopolitan feel mixed with a deep historical soul. It's where old meets new—cobblestone streets leading to contemporary cafes and tech hubs. The Bairro Alto district, with its vibrant nightlife, and the peaceful riverside of Belém, are a few of my favorite spots to spend time in.

Porto, Portugal's second-largest city, is a beautiful mix of ancient architecture and modern growth. Known for its stunning riverside, Porto offers a slower pace than Lisbon but still provides all the amenities of city life. The local wine culture, particularly in Vila Nova de Gaia, across the river, is world-famous. Walking along the Dom Luís I Bridge, you can feel the energy of the city pulsing beneath you, and every time I visit, I discover something new. Whether it's the lively Mercado do Bolhão or the stunning Livraria Lello, there's always something to see or experience in Porto.

Then there's the Algarve, the southernmost region of Portugal, which draws expats in droves. Its sandy beaches, dramatic cliffs, and warm Mediterranean climate make it a magnet for retirees and those seeking a laid-back lifestyle. Cities like Faro, Lagos, and Albufeira are perfect for those looking to live near the ocean, with an abundance of resorts, restaurants, and golf courses. The Algarve offers a more relaxed way of life, with ample sunshine and friendly communities.

Each of these regions has its own distinct charm, but it's important to know what type of lifestyle you want when choosing your home in Portugal. Whether you're drawn to the history and energy of Lisbon, the charm of Porto, or the sunshine of the Algarve, there's a place for everyone.

3.2 Renting vs. Buying Property

One of the first decisions you'll face when looking for a place to live in Portugal is whether to rent or buy property. Both options come with their pros and cons, depending on your long-term plans, financial situation, and the flexibility you want in your move.

Renting in Portugal is quite common, especially for expats who are still figuring out where they want to settle. Rent prices in cities like Lisbon can vary significantly depending on the location and size of the apartment. In Lisbon, rent prices generally rise the closer you are to the city center or the riverfront. A one-bedroom apartment in central Lisbon might cost between €800-€1,200 a month, while further out in neighborhoods like Amadora or Loures, the rent could be half of that.

For those wanting a more peaceful, rural lifestyle, rental prices in towns outside the major cities can be much lower. Smaller towns in the interior, such as Evora or Castelo Branco, offer an entirely different atmosphere at a fraction of the cost. There are also short-term rentals available, perfect for those looking to explore the country before committing to a long-term lease.

On the other hand, buying property is also a great option if you're looking for long-term stability or have a significant budget. Property prices in Portugal have been steadily increasing over the years, especially in Lisbon, Porto, and the Algarve. If you plan to buy in Lisbon's historic center, be prepared for prices in the €3,000-€6,000 per square meter range, depending on the neighborhood.

However, buying property outside the big cities can be much more affordable. In places like Coimbra or the Alentejo, you can find charming homes for a fraction of the cost, often with more space and less crowded surroundings. It's worth noting that Portugal offers a Golden Visa program for foreign investors, which can make purchasing property even more appealing.

3.3 How to Navigate Portugal's Real Estate Market

Navigating the Portuguese real estate market can be a bit daunting, but with some patience and research, it's not as difficult as it may seem. The market is largely regulated, and many transactions are straightforward. However, it's important to understand how the process works before diving in.

For starters, most property listings are available online through sites like Idealista, Imovirtual, and OLX. These platforms provide comprehensive listings in cities and towns across the country, making it easy to search for properties that fit your needs and budget. It's important to be cautious about listings that seem too good to be true—there are scams out there, so always double-check the details.

When you find a property that interests you, it's wise to arrange a visit before making any decisions. If you're not fluent in Portuguese, it might be helpful to work with a real estate agent who speaks your language and can guide you through the process. Agents are often the most reliable resource for navigating the legalities and specifics of buying property.

Once you've found the perfect place, the process for buying property in Portugal generally involves signing a promissory contract (Contrato de Promessa de Compra e Venda) and paying a deposit (usually 10-30% of the purchase price). The full payment is typically made when the final deed (escritura) is signed before a notary.

3.4 Neighborhood Recommendations Based on Lifestyle

When considering where to live in Portugal, the choice of neighborhood is just as important as the city itself. The best neighborhood for you depends on your personal lifestyle, family needs, and career aspirations.

If you're looking for a lively, social atmosphere, the Bairro Alto in Lisbon is a popular expat spot, known for its nightlife and cultural scene. Meanwhile, for families or those seeking tranquility, neighborhoods like Príncipe Real or Areeiro offer a balance of green spaces, quieter streets, and easy access to the city center.

In Porto, the riverside areas near the Dom Luís I Bridge offer scenic views and a buzzing energy, while the more residential areas like Foz or Boavista provide a quieter environment for families or retirees. If you love being near the coast, consider the beachside neighborhoods of Matosinhos or Vila Nova de Gaia, where you can enjoy stunning ocean views without straying too far from city life.

The Algarve, known for its sunny climate, has a number of beach towns and villages perfect for those seeking a slower pace. Tavira, for instance, is an idyllic coastal town with a rich history and relaxed vibe. For those interested in outdoor activities like hiking and golfing, Albufeira or Portimão may be more to your taste.

Before making any big decisions, it's important to familiarize yourself with the legal considerations involved in renting or buying property in Portugal. Portugal has strict property laws, and understanding them will help avoid any surprises along the way.

For renting, tenants have strong legal protections in Portugal, and rental agreements are generally set for one year. Rental contracts can be renewed, and it's customary for landlords to cover property taxes and insurance, while tenants are responsible for utilities. However, ensure that you read the contract carefully to understand your rights and responsibilities.

When buying property, be aware of certain fees that come with the transaction. These can include notary fees, stamp duty, registration costs, and property taxes. It's also important to check that the property has all the necessary certifications, including a certificate of occupancy, proof of land registry, and proof of the property's connection to utilities.

As a foreigner, you'll need a Portuguese taxpayer number (NIF) to sign contracts, open a bank account, and carry out various official procedures.

Many notaries, real estate agents, and lawyers can assist you with this.

CHAPTER 4

Employment Opportunities

Moving to Portugal in 2025 opened my eyes to the array of employment opportunities, especially for those willing to embrace the country's changing economic landscape. As I settled into life here, it became clear that Portugal is increasingly becoming a hub for international talent, digital nomads, and professionals from various fields. Whether you're looking for a corporate job, seeking freelancing opportunities, or considering remote work, Portugal offers something for everyone. Let me walk you through the key industries, navigating the job market, and tips for getting started.

4.1 Industries in Demand

Portugal's economy is diverse, with certain industries experiencing significant growth and demand, particularly in technology, tourism, and agriculture.

Technology and Startups

The tech scene in Portugal has grown exponentially over the past few years. Lisbon, often referred to as the "Silicon Valley of Europe," is home to a thriving startup ecosystem. As a digital nomad myself, I noticed the city's emergence as a hotspot for innovation. Portugal's competitive business environment, alongside government incentives, makes it an attractive place for tech companies to flourish. Fields like software development, digital marketing, AI, cybersecurity, and blockchain are in high demand. If you have a background in any of these areas, you'll find plenty of opportunities.

Tourism and Hospitality

Tourism is one of the pillars of Portugal's economy, and it's clear why—Portugal's stunning landscapes, rich history, and beautiful coastlines attract millions of tourists each year. As I traveled around, it was apparent that the demand for workers in hospitality, tourism management, guiding services, and hotel operations is ever-present. From Lisbon to the Algarve, there's always room for skilled workers in the tourism industry, whether it's as a hotel manager, chef, tour operator, or even as a photographer capturing Portugal's timeless beauty.

Agriculture and Wine

Agriculture, particularly the wine industry, has a longstanding tradition in Portugal. The country's wine-making expertise, particularly in the Douro Valley, has been celebrated worldwide. If you're passionate about agriculture, farming, or the wine industry, you'll find a steady demand for talent in areas ranging from viticulture to marketing and exports. I've visited vineyards and farms that are always on the lookout for experienced workers to help expand their operations.

Renewable Energy

Portugal has taken great strides in advancing its renewable energy capabilities. With an ambitious goal to be carbon-neutral by 2050, the country is leading the charge in wind, solar, and hydropower technologies. If you have a background in renewable energy or sustainability, you'll find a growing number of opportunities here, especially in Lisbon and Porto.

4.2 *Navigating the Job Market*

Navigating the job market in Portugal can be a bit different from what I was used to, but with some patience and the right approach, it's manageable. Here are some tips based on my own experience:

Research and Online Job Portals

Start by browsing job portals like Net-Empregos, Indeed, and LinkedIn. These platforms have a range of opportunities, particularly for professionals in technology, marketing, education, and hospitality. You'll find listings from local and international companies, many of which are open to hiring expats. Some companies even conduct remote interviews in English, which is a huge help for non-Portuguese speakers.

Networking

Networking in Portugal plays a huge role in finding a job. I found that it's not just about sending out resumes but about building relationships. There are numerous expat communities, events, and meetups in Lisbon, Porto, and other cities, where you can meet people in your field. Joining professional networks and attending events is one of the best ways to land a job in Portugal, as many positions are never officially advertised and are filled through word-of-mouth.

Language Skills

While many businesses in Portugal operate in English, particularly in tech and tourism, speaking Portuguese can be a huge advantage. I took a few language classes early on, and it made a difference in my ability to connect with locals and gain access to more job opportunities. Portuguese is often the preferred language in many industries, such as education and government, so learning the basics will give you an edge.

Work Culture

The work culture in Portugal is relaxed but professional. People are generally approachable, and there is a strong focus on maintaining a healthy work-life balance. From what I've observed, companies encourage flexible hours, and there is a clear distinction between personal and professional time. This laid-back approach helps in adapting to the local work environment and finding jobs that allow you to enjoy the beautiful surroundings.

4.3 *How to Obtain a Work Visa*

When I first considered moving to Portugal, the question of how to obtain a work visa loomed large. Thankfully, the process isn't as complicated as I initially thought, but there are a few essential steps to consider.

If you're a non-EU citizen, securing a job offer is a necessary step before you can apply for a work visa. In my case, the employer's role is crucial, as they must apply for your work permit on your behalf. Once approved, the permit allows you to work in Portugal legally. The process may take a few weeks, so I recommend starting well ahead of your desired moving date.

Here are the general steps for obtaining a work visa:

- *Find a Job*: Ensure the job you are applying for is in an area of demand, such as tech, education, or tourism.
- *Secure a Job Offer*: Once you have an offer, your employer will apply for a work permit for you.
- *Submit Documents*: These include your passport, work contract,

qualifications, and proof of accommodation in Portugal.

- *Wait for Approval*: The approval process usually takes a few weeks, but it can vary.

- *Receive Your Visa*: Once granted, you'll be able to travel and start working in Portugal.

I was also aware of the Golden Visa program, which offers a pathway to residency for investors and entrepreneurs willing to invest in Portugal. This program is a fantastic option for those who want to live in Portugal while also making an investment in real estate, business, or job creation.

Networking in Portugal is not just about attending business events, it's about building trust. During my time here, I found that the Portuguese value personal relationships and often do business based on trust and mutual respect.

Here's what worked for me:

- *Join Expats Groups and Forums:* Platforms like Meetup, Facebook groups, and even LinkedIn have communities where expats gather. These groups often share information about job openings and networking events.

- *Attend Industry-Specific Events:* Portugal hosts various tech, tourism, and cultural events throughout the year. These are perfect opportunities to meet people in your industry. I made some valuable contacts by attending conferences and casual meetups.

- *Engage Locally*: Portugal is a country of personal connections. Whether at a café or through a friend of a friend, you'll find that personal connections play a huge role. Don't be afraid to ask locals for advice or introductions.

4.5 Freelancing and Remote Work Opportunities

If you're like me and enjoy the freedom of freelancing, Portugal offers plenty of opportunities, particularly in fields like design, writing, tech, and digital marketing.

The country is becoming a major destination for digital nomads, thanks to its welcoming atmosphere and affordable cost of living. Many expats are setting up businesses or working remotely from the comfort of their homes or co-working spaces. Lisbon and Porto have a thriving community of freelancers, and I was constantly meeting people working for international clients while enjoying the perks of living in such a beautiful country.

Portugal also offers various programs to support freelancers and remote workers, including tax benefits and simplified legal structures for independent contractors. In Lisbon and Porto, co-working spaces like Second Home in Lisbon and Porto i/o in Porto offer flexible workspaces where you can meet like-minded individuals and expand your business or freelance career.

Remote work is certainly on the rise here, and companies are increasingly open to hiring international talent. If you're a freelancer or work remotely, Portugal's infrastructure and expat-friendly atmosphere make it an ideal base.

CHAPTER 5

Navigating Daily Life

5.1 Setting Up Utilities and Internet

When I arrived in Portugal, setting up utilities and the internet was one of the first things I tackled. It's a task that initially seemed daunting, but the process is pretty smooth once you know what to expect.

First, you'll need to decide on the utility providers for electricity, gas, and water. If you're in a major city like Lisbon or Porto, you'll have a variety of options. For electricity, EDP (Electricidade de Portugal) is one of the most common providers. I had to visit their website and choose between a few different plans based on my energy usage, which wasn't hard to figure out. The process of getting connected is relatively quick, and there's an option to handle everything online, though in some cases, you may need to visit their offices for paperwork.

For gas and water, I also used Galp for gas and SMAS for water, both of which offer straightforward services. You'll often need proof of residence, like a rental contract or proof of your address, to set everything up, so have that handy when you go to the provider's office or when registering online.

When it comes to setting up the internet, I had to choose between a few major providers, including MEO, NOS, and Vodafone. All three offer packages for internet, cable TV, and mobile phones, so it's worth looking into all three to find the best deal for you. I opted for MEO, which was incredibly reliable, and the setup process was fairly quick, taking just a few days. One thing to keep in mind is that internet speeds may vary depending on your location—some rural areas can have slower connections, though in most cities, you'll have access to fiber-optic speeds.

In summary, setting up utilities and the internet in Portugal is relatively easy, especially in urban areas. Most services allow you to manage everything online, so there's minimal hassle, just be sure to gather your documents in advance to avoid any delays.

5.2 Public Transportation and Getting Around

Getting around Portugal is surprisingly easy, whether you're in Lisbon, Porto, or one of the smaller towns. The country has a robust public transportation system that includes trains, buses, and trams.

In Lisbon, the Metropolitano de Lisboa (the metro system) is by far the most convenient and affordable way to travel. It's clean, modern, and covers most of the city, from the airport to the suburbs. I used the metro daily, and I found that the Viva Viagem card—rechargeable and valid for both metro and buses—was my best friend. You can load the card at any metro station, and it's valid for unlimited rides on public transport within a specific time period. One thing I learned is that during rush hour, the metro can get packed, so I would plan accordingly if I needed to get somewhere quickly.

In Porto, the Trindade Metro Station is a key hub, and I loved how the metro was integrated with buses and trams. Public transport in Porto is equally efficient, and I often took the historic tram rides along the river, which gave me a charming view of the city.

If you're planning to travel outside of cities, Portugal has a great train network. The Comboios de Portugal service offers frequent and affordable trains to most major cities. I used the train to explore places like Coimbra and the Douro Valley, and I found the rides to be comfortable and scenic, especially along the coast.

For shorter distances, buses are a convenient option. They connect both cities and rural areas. Tickets are inexpensive, and bus stations are easy to navigate. In the Algarve, I relied on buses to get to the beautiful beaches, as they run frequently and are often the best way to get around in more tourist-heavy areas.

Getting around by car is also an option, especially if you're planning to explore the rural countryside or visit remote beaches. The roads in Portugal are generally in good condition, and driving is fairly straightforward. Just be mindful of the toll roads on the highways.

5.3 *Banking in Portugal*

Opening a bank account in Portugal is an essential step to settle in, whether you're working or just need a place to manage your finances. It's not as complicated as I initially thought, but there are a few things to keep in mind. I opened an account with Banco Santander Totta, one of Portugal's largest banks, but there are plenty of other options such as Caixa Geral de Depósitos and Millennium BCP.

You'll need to bring some identification documents, such as your **NIF** (tax identification number, which you'll need for everything from paying taxes to signing a lease), proof of residence, and a passport or European ID card if applicable. The staff at the bank were very helpful in walking me through the process and explaining the different types of accounts available. You'll most likely be offered a "conta à ordem" (current account), which is what I opted for. This type of account allows you to make everyday transactions, like withdrawals, transfers, and bill payments.

A key point is that many banks charge fees for maintaining accounts, although they are generally reasonable. There are also options to avoid fees if you meet certain conditions, like setting up a regular direct deposit or maintaining a minimum balance. For those who want to avoid visiting a branch altogether, many banks offer online services, and I found that managing my account through the bank's mobile app was straightforward and user-friendly.

Having a Portuguese bank account is also crucial for setting up direct debits for your utilities or rent. The process is pretty straightforward, and I was able to manage all my payments without issue.

5.4 *Grocery Shopping and Local Markets*

Grocery shopping in Portugal is one of the simple pleasures of daily life. Whether you're picking up fresh produce at a market or shopping at one of the larger supermarkets, the experience is always enjoyable.

I usually did my grocery shopping at Pingo Doce, one of the country's most popular supermarket chains, which offers a wide variety of goods, from fresh vegetables and meats to international products. I found that the prices were affordable, and the quality of produce was excellent. They also carry a good selection of Portuguese wines and cheeses, which I enjoyed trying out as part of my culinary adventures.

For a more authentic experience, I highly recommend visiting the local markets. In Lisbon, the Mercado da Ribeira (also known as Time Out Market) is a must-see. Not only can you shop for fresh seafood, meats, and cheeses, but you can also enjoy a meal from one of the many food stalls. The market buzzes with energy, offering an authentic glimpse into the heart of Portuguese life.

In Porto, the Mercado do Bolhão is the place to go for fresh produce, flowers, and local specialties. Walking through the market, I was always greeted by friendly vendors offering everything from artisanal bread to locally sourced fish. It's an experience that is as much about the people as it is about the food.

For those in rural areas or smaller towns, there are smaller, more intimate markets, where you can buy fresh fruits, vegetables, and even homemade jams or cured meats. These markets are perfect for getting to know the locals and discovering new flavors unique to each region.

5.5 Integrating Into the Community

One of the most fulfilling aspects of living in Portugal has been the strong sense of community. It's not difficult to integrate, but it does require some effort and openness to new experiences.

I started by learning a bit of Portuguese. While many people speak English, especially in the cities, speaking the language of the country goes a long way in building connections. I enrolled in a language school in Lisbon, and after a few months, I was able to hold conversations with locals at cafés and markets. Portuguese people are warm and friendly, and they truly appreciate it when you make the effort to speak their language.

In addition to language, it's helpful to get involved in local activities and events. Whether it's joining a local group, attending festivals, or simply striking up a conversation with a neighbor, I found that these small efforts made a big difference. Many towns and cities in Portugal host regular cultural festivals, art exhibitions, and outdoor activities, so there's always something going on. I made it a point to participate in local events to experience Portuguese life firsthand.

Volunteering is another great way to integrate. I joined a few community-based projects and made lasting connections while helping out in local food banks and charity events. The Portuguese community is incredibly welcoming, and getting involved not only helped me understand the culture more deeply but also gave me a sense of purpose.

CHAPTER 6

Education and Schools

6.1 Overview of the Portuguese Education System

Having spent considerable time exploring Portugal, I've come to appreciate the country's education system for its structure and diversity.

The Portuguese education system is divided into several stages, beginning with preschool education for children as young as three, which is followed by basic education (Ensino Básico), covering nine years of schooling. This is then followed by secondary education (Ensino Secundário), which lasts for three years and is designed to prepare students for higher education or entering the workforce. The system is largely state-funded, making it highly accessible, and it provides a balanced curriculum that includes subjects like mathematics, science, history, and the arts.

What stands out most to me about the system is how inclusive it is. Students of all backgrounds have access to quality education, and there's a heavy emphasis on promoting critical thinking, creativity, and problem-solving. Schools are well-equipped, and many have recently adopted more modern teaching methods and technologies to keep pace with the evolving world. As I visited a few schools across the country, I noticed that the teachers were passionate about helping their students succeed, and the classroom environments felt engaging and nurturing.

6.2 Public vs. Private Schools

The question of public versus private schooling is a common one for expat families, and it's something I spent some time exploring. Portugal's public schools are free and offer a solid education, making them a viable option for many families. The curriculum in public schools is standardized across the country, with a strong emphasis on Portuguese language and history, as well as foreign languages like English and Spanish. However, public schools can sometimes be overcrowded, especially in larger cities like Lisbon and Porto, which may affect the individual attention students receive.

Private schools, on the other hand, offer smaller class sizes and more personalized attention, but they come at a cost. While private institutions tend to offer a more international approach to education, some also specialize in specific fields, such as the arts or sciences. Many private schools follow international curricula, including the British or American systems, which can be an attractive option for expat families who are planning to stay in Portugal for a limited time.

One of the most compelling reasons people opt for private schooling is the flexibility in languages offered. In private schools, English is often used as the main language of instruction, making the transition easier for children who are not yet fluent in Portuguese. I visited several schools in the Algarve, where private institutions are quite popular due to the large expat community, and found that they often provided a blend of local and international education, preparing students for a globalized world.

6.3 *International Schools for Expats*

For those of us who are moving to Portugal from abroad, the idea of enrolling children in an international school can feel like the perfect solution. International schools are scattered across the country, but there's a high concentration in larger cities like Lisbon, Porto, and Cascais. These schools are designed to cater to expat families, providing curricula that align with educational systems from around the world, such as the British, American, or French systems.

What I appreciate most about international schools is the seamless integration of global perspectives into the classroom. Children from all corners of the world interact in a multicultural environment, which fosters cross-cultural understanding and communication. These schools often offer advanced language programs and extracurricular activities, which can help expat children adjust while still being exposed to the cultural richness of their new home.

In Lisbon, for example, the International School of Lisbon offers an

American curriculum and attracts students from various countries. Similarly, in Porto, the Oporto British School provides a British-style education that's highly regarded for its academic rigor and focus on extracurricular development. Having visited several of these institutions, I was impressed by their well-rounded approach to education, where students are encouraged not only to excel academically but also to participate in sports, arts, and community service projects.

6.4 Higher Education and Universities

Portugal has a long tradition of academic excellence, with universities that rank among the best in Europe. From my time in Portugal, it's clear that the country is home to some remarkable institutions that offer a wide array of undergraduate and postgraduate programs. The University of Lisbon, for instance, is not only one of the largest but also one of the most prestigious, with a strong reputation in areas like engineering, law, and the sciences. Similarly, Universidade do Porto offers world-class research opportunities and is well-regarded for its programs in architecture, arts, and health sciences.

One of the things I find particularly appealing about Portuguese universities is their emphasis on research and innovation. Several institutions collaborate with international universities, providing students with opportunities to participate in groundbreaking studies and projects. If you're planning to study in Portugal, you'll find that there's a wealth of options, whether you're looking for a top-tier academic experience or an institution with a strong international focus.

As someone who has spent time both studying and living in Portugal, I can vouch for the welcoming nature of its higher education institutions. The universities are open to international students, and many of the programs are offered in English, which makes it an easy transition for non-Portuguese speakers. Most universities also offer a variety of scholarships, especially for postgraduate students, making higher education in Portugal both accessible and affordable for many international students.

Learning Portuguese has been one of the most rewarding challenges of my time in Portugal, and I've found that there are numerous resources available to help newcomers get up to speed. If you're planning to live in Portugal for an extended period, it's highly recommended to learn the language, as it'll allow you to better integrate into the local culture and community.

For those who prefer formal instruction, there are many language schools that offer Portuguese language courses, ranging from beginner to advanced levels. Cial Centro de Linguas, based in Lisbon, offers high-quality language programs that focus on both conversation and grammar. Another great resource is Lisbon Language School, where I took a beginner's course upon arrival. The classes were immersive and helped me gain a solid foundation in Portuguese, especially the essential vocabulary and grammar needed for everyday life.

If you're looking for more flexibility, online resources are plentiful. Websites like Duolingo and Babbel have interactive apps that allow you to practice Portuguese at your own pace, making it a great option for busy individuals. For those wanting to take it a step further, Pimsleur offers audio lessons that allow you to learn while commuting or going about daily tasks. I personally found these to be helpful for improving pronunciation and comprehension, especially when speaking with locals.

Additionally, immersion is key. I recommend seeking out language exchange groups, where you can meet locals who want to practice English while you learn Portuguese. It's a fantastic way to get comfortable with conversational Portuguese and pick up colloquial phrases that you won't necessarily learn in a classroom setting. I joined a few exchange groups in Lisbon, and it not only helped me improve my language skills but also gave me the chance to make friends and feel more connected to the community.

CHAPTER 7

Tourist Attractions in Portugal

7.1 *Lisbon's Historic Belém Tower*

When I think of Lisbon, the first image that comes to mind is the iconic Belém Tower (Torre de Belém), a symbol of the city's rich maritime history. Nestled along the Tagus River, this 16th-century fortress was originally built to defend the city's harbor. As I wandered through its narrow stone passageways and climbed to the top, I couldn't help but be transported back in time, imagining the ships that sailed from here to discover new worlds. The tower's intricate Manueline architecture, with its ornate decorations and views overlooking the river, is nothing short of breathtaking.

Located in the Belém district, which is known for its historical significance, the tower is an essential stop for anyone visiting Lisbon. I often found myself walking along the riverbank just to enjoy the sight of it. There's a peaceful serenity around the tower, and the surrounding gardens make it the perfect place to relax. Just a short walk away is the famous Jerónimos Monastery, another UNESCO World Heritage site, and the Monument to the Discoveries, both of which tie into Portugal's Age of Exploration.

7.2 The Dom Luís I Bridge and Ribeira Neighborhood in Porto

Porto is a city that captured my heart from the moment I crossed the Dom Luís I Bridge. This magnificent double-deck iron bridge, designed by a student of Gustave Eiffel, spans the Douro River, connecting Porto with Vila Nova de Gaia. The views from the bridge are incredible, offering a panoramic glimpse of Porto's terracotta rooftops and the winding streets of the Ribeira District below.

Ribeira, Porto's oldest district, is a maze of narrow, cobbled streets lined with colorful houses. I spent hours here, wandering past quaint cafés, charming boutiques, and traditional restaurants where the scent of grilled sardines filled the air. There's a certain old-world charm to Ribeira that makes it feel like stepping into another era. One of my favorite activities was taking a boat ride along the Douro River to see Porto from a different angle. At night, the bridge lights up, creating a magical scene that I'll never forget.

7.3 Sinatra's Fairy Tale Palaces

Sintra, only a brief train journey from Lisbon, resembles a scene straight out of a fairy tale. The town is set against the backdrop of the lush Sintra mountains, and as I walked through its winding streets, I was constantly amazed by the stunning palaces and castles that dotted the landscape. Pena Palace, with its bright yellow and red façade, is perhaps the most famous, standing proudly atop a hill with views that stretch for miles. The palace is a delightful mix of architectural styles, from Gothic to

Renaissance, and I spent hours exploring its rooms and gardens.

Just a few minutes away is Quinta da Regaleira, a mystical estate filled with hidden gardens, caves, and a remarkable initiation well. The well's spiral staircase descends into the earth, and I couldn't resist the urge to descend, imagining myself in the footsteps of secret societies that once used it for their rituals. Sinatra's atmosphere is magical, and I highly recommend visiting it for a day trip or, if you have the time, staying overnight to experience its tranquil beauty.

7.4 *Algarve's Stunning Beaches*

The Algarve, Portugal's southernmost region, is home to some of the most stunning beaches I've ever seen. From the golden sands and crystal-clear waters to the dramatic cliffs and hidden caves, the Algarve offers something for every beach lover. My favorite beach by far was Praia da Marinha, often listed as one of the most beautiful beaches in the world. The cliffs that rise from the beach are striking, and the waters are calm, making it perfect for swimming or simply relaxing by the sea.

Beyond the beaches, the Algarve also boasts charming coastal towns such as Lagos, Albufeira, and Tavira, each offering its own unique blend of history, culture, and local cuisine. I spent many afternoons in Lagos, strolling through its cobbled streets, enjoying freshly grilled sardines, and taking in the lively yet relaxed atmosphere. Whether you're looking for adventure, relaxation, or both, the Algarve's beaches will not disappoint.

7.5 Douro Valley's Wine Country

One of the most unforgettable experiences I had in Portugal was visiting the Douro Valley, the heart of the country's wine production. The valley, which stretches along the Douro River, is a UNESCO World Heritage site and offers some of the most stunning views I've ever encountered. Rolling vineyards, terraced hillsides, and charming villages dot the landscape, and as I toured some of the region's famous wine estates, I learned about the centuries-old tradition of port wine production.

One particular estate, Quinta do Vallado, left a lasting impression on me. The estate dates back to 1716, and its vineyards produce some of the finest port wines in Portugal. I had the privilege of tasting some of their best offerings while overlooking the valley. The experience was both educational and sensory, as I learned about the winemaking process and enjoyed the distinct flavors of the region's wines.

7.6 *The Medieval City of Óbidos*

Óbidos, a medieval town located about an hour north of Lisbon, is one of the most picturesque places I visited in Portugal. The town is encircled by well-preserved walls, and as I walked through its narrow streets, I couldn't help but feel like I had stepped back in time. The cobbled streets are lined with whitewashed houses adorned with colorful flowers, and the town's centerpiece is its impressive castle, Castelo de Óbidos, which dates back to the 12th century.

Óbidos is also famous for its cherry liqueur, ginjinha, and I made sure to stop at one of the local shops to try a glass. The town is incredibly charming, and every corner seemed to offer a new photo opportunity. The best part about Óbidos is that it remains relatively uncrowded compared to other tourist destinations, making it the perfect spot for a relaxing day trip or a romantic getaway.

7.7 Madeira Island's Scenic Beauty

Madeira Island, often referred to as the "Island of Eternal Spring," is a paradise for nature lovers, and I couldn't wait to explore its stunning landscapes. Located in the Atlantic Ocean, off the coast of North Africa, Madeira offers everything from lush forests and towering cliffs to volcanic peaks and serene beaches. I spent several days hiking through the

Laurisilva Forest, a UNESCO World Heritage site, where I marveled at the ancient trees and diverse plant life.

One of the highlights of my trip was visiting Monte, a hilltop village overlooking Funchal, the capital of Madeira. I took a traditional toboggan ride down the hill, a unique experience that was both thrilling and fun. Madeira's scenery is breathtaking, and whether you're hiking, exploring botanical gardens, or simply soaking in the views from a cliffside restaurant, the island offers a peaceful retreat from the hustle and bustle of mainland Portugal.

7.8 The Azores Archipelago

The Azores, a group of nine volcanic islands located in the North Atlantic, are often overlooked by tourists, which is one of the reasons I was drawn to them. These islands offer some of the most untouched, dramatic landscapes I've ever seen. São Miguel, the largest island, is home to stunning crater lakes, lush green hills, and hot springs. I visited Sete Cidades, a picturesque village nestled between two volcanic lakes, and was awe-struck by the beauty of the surrounding landscape.

The Azores are perfect for those looking for adventure. I hiked across volcanic terrain, swam in hot springs, and even went whale watching. The islands are known for their biodiversity, and the waters surrounding the Azores are one of the best places in the world to spot whales and dolphins. If you're looking for an off-the-beaten-path destination with natural beauty at its core, the Azores is the place to go.

7.9 Coimbra's Historic University

Coimbra, one of Portugal's oldest cities, is home to the prestigious University of Coimbra, which dates back to 1290. As I walked through the university's historic buildings, I could feel the weight of centuries of academic tradition. The university is not just a place of learning but also a tourist attraction, with highlights like the Joanina Library, a stunning Baroque building filled with ancient manuscripts and books.

The city itself is filled with charming streets, picturesque gardens, and beautiful architecture. One of my favorite spots was the Portugal dos Pequenitos, a miniature park that showcases the country's most iconic buildings in tiny scale. Coimbra's rich history and youthful energy, due to the large student population, make it a fascinating place to visit.

7.10 *Évora's Roman Temple and Chapel of Bones*

Évora, a UNESCO World Heritage site in the Alentejo region, is a town brimming with history. One of the highlights of my visit was the Roman Temple of Évora, a stunning 2,000-year-old structure that stands in the heart of the city. The temple's well-preserved columns are a testament to the town's Roman past, and standing before them felt like stepping back in time.

Just a short walk from the temple is the Chapel of Bones (Capela dos Ossos), an eerie but fascinating site. The chapel is decorated with the bones and skulls of over 5,000 people, a reminder of the transient nature of life. While it's a bit macabre, the chapel's historical significance cannot be overstated. Évora is a town where history is alive around every corner, making it an essential stop for any history enthusiast.

CHAPTER 8

Accommodations

8A: *Overview of Accommodation Options*

When it comes to choosing where to stay in Portugal, you truly have an abundance of options that can cater to every taste, budget, and preference. From swanky beach resorts on the Algarve to charming boutique hotels tucked away in Lisbon's cobbled streets, Portugal has something for everyone. If you're after the luxury experience, Portugal's coastal regions are dotted with high-end resorts. But if you prefer something more quaint, the countryside is brimming with beautiful villas, rustic farmhouses, and even luxurious glamping sites. Whether you seek relaxation, adventure, or cultural immersion, Portugal's accommodations are as diverse as its landscape.

8B: *Luxury Resorts*

When I think of the ultimate indulgence in Portugal, my mind immediately drifts to the luxury resorts that line the golden shores of the Algarve. One of my most unforgettable stays was at Vila Vita Parc Resort in Porches. Tucked away between cliffs and the Atlantic Ocean, this resort offers more than just a place to rest your head. With private villas, Michelin-star dining, and an award-winning spa, it felt as if every detail was designed to pamper and spoil. The views from the resort's terraces are simply spectacular, offering an endless expanse of ocean meeting the sky. It's not just the location that makes this place unforgettable but the impeccable service, where every need is anticipated before you even think to ask.

Another gem I've experienced is Pine Cliffs Resort near Albufeira. This place truly feels like a retreat from the outside world. Set in a pine forest with access to a private beach, it's a perfect blend of nature and luxury. The resort also has top-tier golf courses and a variety of fine dining options. The spaciousness and serenity here really make it easy to unwind and feel pampered.

8C: *Budget-Friendly Hotels*

While luxury resorts offer an unparalleled experience, I've found that Portugal also excels when it comes to budget-friendly hotels that provide comfort and style without breaking the bank. For instance, Lisbon's Hotel Real Parque is a true hidden gem. Located in the heart of the city, it's close to metro stations, making it a great base for exploring. With clean, modern rooms and a lovely breakfast spread, it offers fantastic value for money.

For those heading to Porto, Moov Hotel Porto Norte offers contemporary accommodations at a reasonable price. Situated slightly outside the historic center, this hotel provides easy access to public transport and has an inviting, minimalist design. The real highlight for me was the hotel's eco-conscious approach, with energy-efficient systems and a commitment to sustainability. It's the ideal mix of comfort, value, and eco-consciousness.

If you crave something more personalized, Portugal's boutique hotels are a wonderful way to experience the country's charm in style. One hotel I truly love is the Bairro Alto Hotel in Lisbon. Nestled in the heart of the city's lively Bairro Alto district, this small hotel blends old-world charm with sleek, modern amenities. The staff truly make you feel at home, offering insider tips about the city that most tourists miss. What sets this place apart is its rooftop terrace, where you can sip a cocktail and look out over the city's rooftops while the sun sets in a kaleidoscope of colors.

Another fantastic boutique experience I had was at The House of Sandeman in Porto. Situated in the historic cellars of Sandeman, this hotel allows guests to immerse themselves in the world of Port wine. The design combines rustic charm with modern elegance, and the views of the Douro River are simply stunning. It's a wonderful base for exploring the nearby wine cellars and the charming Ribeira district, where I spent hours just wandering the cobblestone streets and soaking in the beauty of the city.

For a truly unique experience, consider stepping away from the typical hotel scene and staying in one of Portugal's stunning villas or farmhouses. On a trip to the Alentejo region, I stayed at a traditional Portuguese farmhouse, and it was an unforgettable experience. The farmhouse, Monte da Serralheira, was tucked into the rolling hills of the countryside, offering views of olive groves and vineyards stretching as far as the eye could see. The home was rustic yet beautifully renovated, combining old-world charm with modern comforts. The real highlight for me, though, was the opportunity to live like a local—waking up to the sounds of nature, sipping coffee on the terrace, and enjoying homemade regional dishes.

If you're craving something a bit more adventurous, Portugal is also home to some of Europe's best glamping sites. One such place, Vilar Rural de Cerveira, offers luxury tents surrounded by nature, close to the border with Spain. With comfortable bedding, private bathrooms, and an outdoor patio, it's the perfect way to connect with nature while enjoying modern amenities. The experience is very much about balance—being enveloped by the tranquility of the countryside but still having access to the finer comforts of life.

8F: Top Recommended Accommodations

Throughout my travels, there were certain accommodations that stood out, not just for their comfort, but for their sense of place and the experiences they offered. The Yeatman Hotel in Porto, for instance, is more than just a five-star hotel—it's an experience. The property is perched on the hills above the city, offering magnificent panoramic views of the Porto skyline and the Douro River. The hotel has a Michelin-star restaurant, and the wine cellar, which boasts an impressive collection of Portuguese wines, is an experience in itself. The rooms are spacious, elegant, and designed with an eye for comfort, but it's the stunning views and the world-class service that will make your stay unforgettable.

In Lisbon, Santa Clara 1728 was another standout for me. This boutique hotel, located in a restored 17th-century convent, feels more like staying in a private home than a hotel. The decor is a beautiful mix of modern and historical elements, and the service is personal and attentive. What makes it special is the intimate feel, combined with its central location, which allowed me to easily explore the Alfama district and beyond.

Choosing the right accommodation in Portugal really comes down to your priorities. If luxury is what you seek, you won't be disappointed by the high-end resorts in places like the Algarve or the Lisbon coast. However, if you're more of an adventurer and want a truly unique stay, the countryside offers many charming villas, farmhouses, and even glamping experiences.

For those on a budget, there are plenty of excellent, budget-friendly options that offer great value. Lisbon and Porto have an abundance of affordable hotels with easy access to public transport and all the attractions these cities offer. And let's not forget the boutique hotels, which are perfect for those who want something personal and stylish while exploring Portugal's hidden gems.

Think about what matters most to you: Is it the location, the amenities, the experience, or the price? Portugal offers so much in terms of accommodations, so no matter your style or budget, there's something here for everyone.

8H: *Booking Tips and Tricks*

When it comes to booking your stay in Portugal, flexibility is key. Portugal is one of those destinations where the best accommodations can often be found when you book early, especially in the peak summer months. If you have a set location in mind, booking months in advance will give you the best chance of securing your preferred choice.

For the budget-conscious traveler, it's always worth checking out booking websites like Booking.com and Airbnb for special deals or last-minute offers. Don't forget to read reviews—there's nothing quite like hearing firsthand experiences from fellow travelers to help guide your decision. Many hotels in Portugal also offer discounts or perks for longer stays, so if you're planning to spend a few weeks or more, it's definitely worth asking about special offers.

CHAPTER 9

Itineraries

When it comes to experiencing Portugal, planning the right itinerary can make all the difference. Whether you're escaping for a weekend, seeking a deeper cultural connection, or crafting a romantic escape, Portugal offers a palette of adventures to suit every traveler's desires. Having spent a significant amount of time exploring its hidden gems and renowned landmarks, I can confidently guide you through thoughtfully curated plans. Each itinerary below reflects the richness of Portugal's culture, landscapes, and warm hospitality.

9A *Weekend Getaways*

For a quick but meaningful trip, Portugal's cities and surrounding countryside offer endless charm.

- *Lisbon and Cascais*: Start your weekend in Lisbon with a tram ride through the Alfama district, savoring the city's historic architecture and traditional Fado music echoing through its cobblestone streets. Make sure to visit the Time Out Market for a taste of Portugal's contemporary culinary scene. On the second day, take a short drive or train to Cascais. Here, the golden beaches and laid-back vibe provide the perfect respite. Don't miss Boca do Inferno, a dramatic coastal cliff formation that will leave you awestruck.

- *Porto and Douro Valley*: Begin in Porto's Ribeira district, with its colorful facades and lively riverfront cafes. Spend the evening sampling local dishes and sipping Port wine. The next day, journey to the Douro Valley, where terraced vineyards roll endlessly. A wine-tasting tour aboard a river cruise is a highlight not to be missed.

Portugal's rich history and traditions make it a playground for culture enthusiasts.

- *Sintra's Palaces*: Spend an entire day in Sintra, a UNESCO World Heritage Site. Wander through the whimsical Pena Palace, the Moorish Castle, and the romantic Quinta da Regaleira, with its intricate gardens and mystical wells.

- *Coimbra*: This historic city is home to one of the oldest universities in the world. The Baroque Joanina Library is a feast for the eyes, and the city's medieval streets invite leisurely exploration. In the evening, treat yourself to a Fado performance unique to Coimbra's heritage.

- *Évora*: A treasure trove of Roman, Gothic, and Manueline architecture. Visit the Chapel of Bones, an eerie yet fascinating landmark, and savor the hearty Alentejo cuisine at a local tavern.

9C *Outdoor Adventure*

Nature lovers will find Portugal an exhilarating playground for outdoor activities.

- *Peneda-Gerês National Park*: Located in the north, this park boasts lush forests, sparkling waterfalls, and abundant wildlife. Hiking trails lead to stunning vistas and ancient Roman ruins scattered throughout the park.

- *Serra da Estrela*: If you're visiting in winter, this is Portugal's prime destination for skiing. During the warmer months, it transforms into a hiker's paradise, with trails winding through granite peaks and serene lakes.

- *Adores*: The islands offer otherworldly volcanic landscapes, crater lakes, and endless opportunities for hiking, whale watching, and kayaking. São Miguel's Sete Cidades is particularly breathtaking.

9D Family-Friendly Trips

Portugal's welcoming nature extends to families, making it an excellent choice for all ages.

- *Lagos and Algarve Beaches*: With calm waters and soft sands, beaches like Meia Praia and Praia Dona Ana are ideal for kids. The Ponta da Piedade cliffs add an adventurous touch to your family trip.

- *Lisbon Zoo*: Nestled in the heart of Lisbon, the zoo offers an engaging day out. Its cable car ride provides unique views of the park's residents and the city beyond.

- *Oceanário de Lisboa*: This world-class aquarium is a hit with children and adults alike. Featuring a massive central tank, it showcases marine life from the Atlantic, Pacific, Indian, and Antarctic oceans.

9E Budget Travel

Portugal is known for being one of Europe's most affordable destinations, and traveling on a budget doesn't mean sacrificing quality experiences.

- *Stay in Pousadas*: Portugal's network of affordable guesthouses and converted monasteries, like those in Óbidos and Marvão, provide cozy accommodations at great prices.
- *Public Transportation*: Take advantage of Portugal's extensive train and bus networks to explore cities like Porto and Lisbon without breaking the bank.
- *Street Food and Markets*: Sample local delicacies such as bifanas, pasteis de nata, and grilled sardines at local

markets like Mercado da Ribeira in Lisbon or Bolhão Market in Porto.

Traveling solo in Portugal is a liberating experience, with its safe environment and friendly locals making it easy to connect with people.

- *Explore Porto*: Porto's walkable streets, lively cafes, and welcoming hostels make it an ideal destination for solo travelers. Engage in a wine-tasting tour and enjoy the city's vibrant energy.
- *Yoga Retreats in the Algarve*: Balance adventure with self-care by joining a yoga retreat. The Algarve's sun-soaked

coastline and tranquil settings are perfect for rejuvenation.

- *Join Group Tours*: Whether it's a guided hike in the Douro Valley or a cooking class in Lisbon, group activities provide a wonderful opportunity to meet like-minded travelers.

9G *Romantic Getaways*

Portugal's landscapes and historic charm create a romantic atmosphere for couples seeking an unforgettable escape.

- *Madeira's Secluded Beauty*: The island of Madeira is a sanctuary for couples. Enjoy a stay at a luxurious cliffside resort, take a leisurely walk along the Levadas (irrigation channels), and share a bottle of Madeira wine while watching the sunset over the Atlantic.

- *Alentejo's Countryside*: With its rolling hills, golden plains, and quaint villages, Alentejo offers a quiet, intimate retreat. Stay at a traditional winery estate and enjoy candlelit dinners under starry skies.

- *Sinatra's Romantic Places*: The fairytale allure of Sintra makes it a perfect destination for couples. Wander through the lush gardens of Monserrate Palace and steal a kiss at the breathtaking Pena Palace.

CHAPTER 10

Portugal's Political and Social Landscape

10.1 The Current President of Portugal

Spending time in Portugal has allowed me to develop a deep appreciation for its leadership, and President Marcelo Rebelo de Sousa stands as an emblematic figure of the nation. Often referred to as "the President of Affection" by locals, he exudes a remarkable warmth and accessibility rarely seen in global politics. Whether walking the streets of Cascais, where he is known to chat freely with locals, or attending cultural events across the country, his presence feels less like a political figurehead and more like a beloved neighbor.

Marcelo's presidency, which began in 2016, has been marked by his dedication to uniting the Portuguese people. His approachable demeanor hides a sharp intellect; he is a former professor of law at the University of Lisbon and a respected political analyst. Known for his impartial stance, he emphasizes consensus and national unity, often mediating between political factions. You can see his influence in the way ordinary citizens discuss politics with an unusual blend of respect and engagement.

His efforts in modern diplomacy have also earned him respect on the international stage. One memorable moment for me was visiting the Presidential Palace, Palácio de Belém, at Praça Afonso de Albuquerque in Lisbon. The history there feels alive, intertwined with Marcelo's efforts to balance Portugal's storied past with the demands of contemporary governance.

10.2 Overview of the Political System

Portugal's political system is a fascinating blend of history and modernity. The country operates as a semi-presidential republic, where power is shared between the President, the Prime Minister, and the Assembly of the Republic. As a visitor who's spent time exploring both urban hubs and rural areas, I've witnessed how this system impacts daily life.

The Prime Minister, currently António Costa, leads the government, focusing on the nation's day-to-day operations. Costa's tenure has been defined by pragmatic economic policies, often rooted in his Socialist Party's progressive stance. The Parliament, located at Palácio de São Bento on Rua de São Bento in Lisbon, acts as the legislative branch. Its imposing neoclassical architecture reflects the weight of the decisions made within its halls. If you're lucky, you might catch a glimpse of heated debates, which are open to public viewing on certain days.

Portugal's Constitution, adopted in 1976, is a modern document that emphasizes human rights, equality, and democracy, a clear reflection of the country's post-revolutionary ethos. The Carnation Revolution of 1974, which ended decades of dictatorship, still lingers in the collective memory of the people. Walking through the streets of Lisbon, you'll find murals and statues commemorating this pivotal moment, like the Carnation Monument at Largo do Carmo.

Elections in Portugal are vibrant civic events. The President is elected every five years through a direct vote, while parliamentary elections determine the composition of the Assembly. Proportional representation ensures diverse voices are heard, creating a robust democratic dialogue.

10.3 Portugal's Role in the European Union

One cannot understand modern Portugal without examining its role within the European Union. Since joining the EU in 1986, the country has transformed, leveraging membership to boost its infrastructure, economy, and global standing. I remember standing at

Praça do Comércio in Lisbon, gazing at the Tagus River, and reflecting on Portugal's journey from a maritime empire to an integral part of a united Europe.

Portugal's commitment to the EU is evident in its leadership roles. The country hosted the rotating presidency of the Council of the European Union in 2021, steering key discussions on sustainability, digital transformation, and the post-COVID-19 recovery. During my visit to the Palácio Nacional da Ajuda in Lisbon, where some EU meetings were held, I was struck by the historic backdrop juxtaposed with the forward-looking agenda of these discussions.

Economically, the EU has been a lifeline for Portugal. Structural funds have revamped the nation's infrastructure, from highways connecting remote villages to urban development projects like the Parque das Nações district in Lisbon. However, membership is not without its challenges. The 2008 financial crisis tested the country's resolve, leading to austerity measures that reshaped public perception of the EU.

Portugal's strategic position at the southwestern edge of Europe also makes it a key player in transatlantic relations. The port city of Sines, for instance, has become a vital hub for LNG imports and digital connectivity, hosting major undersea cables linking Europe to the Americas.

10.4 Social Initiatives and Sustainability Efforts

Portugal's commitment to social welfare and sustainability is deeply woven into its national identity. Walking through the Alfama district in Lisbon or the Ribeira neighborhood in Porto, I've seen firsthand how the government's initiatives are designed to uplift communities while preserving cultural heritage.

One notable effort is the Programa de Renda Acessível, an affordable housing program aimed at addressing the housing crisis in urban areas. The beautifully restored buildings along Avenida da Liberdade in Lisbon are a testament to the delicate balance between modernization and preservation. These projects prioritize affordability while respecting the architectural soul of the cities.

In sustainability, Portugal is a leader. The country generates over 60% of its electricity from renewable sources, including wind, solar, and hydropower. During a visit to the Alto Minho wind farm in Viana do Castelo, I marveled at the towering turbines that symbolize Portugal's renewable energy ambitions. Additionally, the small town of Porto

Santo in Madeira is pioneering a "Smart Fossil-Free Island" initiative, aiming to eliminate its reliance on non-renewable energy.

Portugal's social programs also emphasize education and health. The Serviço Nacional de Saúde (SNS) provides universal health care, which I've seen locals praise for its accessibility, though challenges remain in reducing wait times and ensuring resources for rural areas. Visiting the Universidade de Coimbra, one of the oldest universities in the world, I was reminded of Portugal's enduring commitment to education as a tool for social mobility.

The government also promotes gender equality and LGBTQ+ rights, making Portugal one of the most progressive countries in Southern Europe. Events like Lisbon Pride, held annually in Marquês de Pombal, highlight the inclusive spirit of the nation. On the streets, you feel a sense of openness and acceptance that resonates deeply with locals and visitors alike.

Portugal's dedication to sustainability extends to its agricultural practices. The Alentejo region, known for its olive groves and vineyards, has embraced organic farming methods. During a wine-tasting tour at Herdade do Esporão near Reguengos de Monsaraz, I learned how local producers balance tradition with eco-conscious innovation, ensuring the land remains fertile for generations.

CHAPTER 11

Sustainability and Conservation

Portugal is more than its stunning landscapes, cultural heritage, and cuisine. It's a country leading the charge in sustainability and conservation efforts, blending innovation with a deep respect for its natural resources. Having spent a significant amount of time exploring the country's initiatives and landscapes, I can say firsthand that Portugal's commitment to environmental stewardship is nothing short of remarkable.

11.1 Portugal's Green Energy Policies

Portugal's approach to renewable energy is visionary, and its achievements are a testament to this ambition. The country has set an example by investing heavily in wind, solar, and hydroelectric power. I was amazed to learn that in certain years, Portugal generated as much as 60% of its energy from renewable sources. As you travel through the countryside, you'll notice fields dotted with wind turbines, particularly in regions like Alentejo and Oeste.

One memorable trip was to the Sobral Monte Agraço Wind Farm, located near Lisbon. You can reach it by heading towards the municipality of Sobral de

Monte Agraço along the A8 highway. The site itself, surrounded by rolling green hills, is a quiet yet powerful reminder of Portugal's commitment to clean energy. Standing there, with the turbines humming softly against a backdrop of blue skies, I felt an odd sense of awe—technology and nature working in harmony.

Solar energy is another area where Portugal shines, quite literally. I recall visiting a solar farm near Moura, in Alentejo, a region known for its vast plains and sunlit days. The farm, officially called the "Moura Photovoltaic Power Station," sits just outside the town, about an hour's drive from Évora. The endless rows of solar panels seem to stretch infinitely, a futuristic landscape that promises a cleaner tomorrow.

Even urban areas showcase Portugal's commitment. Lisbon has been integrating solar panels into public transport and lighting. During my time there, I noticed how commonplace electric car charging stations were, a sign of the country's push towards reducing carbon emissions.

11.2 Protected National Parks and Reserves

Portugal's natural beauty is as diverse as it is breathtaking, and its network of national parks and reserves ensures that future generations can enjoy these treasures. One of my favorite spots is Peneda-Gerês National Park, located in the north, near Braga. Enter the park through the village of Campo do Gerês, where you'll find the entrance gates leading to a world of untouched beauty.

Peneda-Gerês isn't just a park; it's a sanctuary. The towering granite peaks, gushing waterfalls like Arado Falls, and serene lakes such as Vilarinho das Furnas are mesmerizing. I spent hours wandering along trails like the Mata da Albergaria, enveloped by ancient oak trees and the soft rustle of wildlife. You might even spot Iberian wolves or wild ponies if you're lucky.

Heading south, the Ria Formosa Natural Park, near Faro in the Algarve, offers a completely different yet equally captivating experience. The park spans several towns, but I found myself enchanted by the salt marshes near Olhão. You can rent a bike or take a boat tour from the marina in Olhão, weaving through lagoons and learning about the local flora and fauna. Flamingos, storks, and other migratory birds are abundant, their graceful movements adding life to the calm waters.

For something unique, the Laurisilva Forest in Madeira, a UNESCO World Heritage site, feels like stepping into another world. Located in the northern parts of the island, this subtropical forest thrives in the humid climate. I entered through the town of Santana, and as I ventured deeper, the air grew cooler, the trees taller, their moss-covered trunks whispering stories of centuries past. It's a stark reminder of the importance of preserving such rare ecosystems.

11.3 How Expats Can Contribute to Sustainability Efforts

Living in Portugal as an expat, I quickly realized that sustainability isn't just a national initiative—it's a community-driven effort. There's a shared sense of responsibility, and expats can play a significant role in these efforts.

One of the simplest yet impactful actions is supporting local markets. Every Saturday, I visit the Mercado Biológico do Príncipe Real in Lisbon's Príncipe Real neighborhood. It's an open-air market where local farmers sell organic produce, honey, and artisanal goods. By buying local, expats can reduce their carbon footprint and support sustainable farming practices.

Another way to contribute is by embracing Portugal's excellent public transport system. I've often relied on the trains run by CP – Comboios de Portugal to travel between cities. For shorter trips, the tram network in Lisbon or the eco-friendly buses in Porto are fantastic. Reducing car usage not only cuts emissions but also allows you to experience the country at a slower, more intimate pace.

For those with a green thumb, volunteering with reforestation projects is a meaningful way to give back. After the devastating wildfires in central Portugal, several organizations, such as Plantar uma Árvore, have been working tirelessly to restore native forests. I once joined a group planting trees near Pedrógão Grande, and the experience was both humbling and rewarding.

Expats can also engage with local conservation groups. In the Algarve, I became involved with a marine conservation project focused on protecting seagrass meadows. We worked from Olhão's marina, diving to study the underwater ecosystem and clean up plastic waste. These efforts not only help preserve marine life but also foster connections with the local community.

Finally, adopting sustainable practices in daily life can make a difference. Many towns and cities have started implementing composting programs, such as the Lisboa Compostar initiative in Lisbon. By composting food waste, expats can contribute to reducing landfill usage and improving soil health.

Portugal's sustainability journey is inspiring, and being part of it has deepened my appreciation for the country. Each initiative, whether it's on a national or community level, carries a sense of urgency and optimism. Walking through its parks, participating in conservation projects, or simply using solar-powered street lights at night, I'm constantly reminded of the balance Portugal strives to maintain between progress and preservation.

CHAPTER 12

Appendix

Traveling through Portugal is an adventure filled with beauty and discovery, but having reliable information at hand can transform a trip from simply enjoyable to truly unforgettable. This chapter serves as a compass, guiding travelers to essential resources, local gems, and practical tools to navigate the country with ease.

12A Emergency Contacts

It's always wise to have key emergency contacts handy when exploring. Portugal has a centralized emergency number—112—which connects to police, fire services, and medical aid.

For specific medical emergencies, I have relied on the Hospital Santa Maria in Lisbon, one of the largest hospitals in the country. Located at Av. Prof. Egas Moniz, 1649-035 Lisbon, this hospital offers 24-hour emergency care and is known for its efficient services.

For tourists requiring English-speaking police assistance, I've found the Tourist Police Station in Lisbon helpful. They are located at Praça dos Restauradores, 1250-096 Lisbon, conveniently near the center of the city.

Traveling through Portugal, I've come to appreciate a mix of traditional maps and modern navigation tools. While apps like Google Maps and Waze are reliable, they sometimes miss the charm of hidden paths in historic neighborhoods.

In Porto, I picked up a beautifully illustrated map from Livraria Lello, located at R. das Carmelitas 144, 4050-161 Porto. This map not only guided me through the city but also highlighted cultural landmarks and lesser-known viewpoints.

For hiking, particularly in Peneda-Gerês National Park, I recommend obtaining detailed trail maps from local visitor centers. The park office at Campo do Gerês offers excellent printed guides that provide insights into elevation and natural highlights.

12C *Additional Reading and References*

To understand Portugal's culture and history, I immersed myself in books that brought the country to life. One gem I found was José Saramago's Journey to Portugal, a poetic exploration of the nation's landscapes and spirit.

For a deeper dive into the history of Lisbon, I recommend Fernando Pessoa's The Book of Disquiet. Copies are readily available at Fnac Chiado, located at Largo do Chiado 5, 1200-108 Lisbon.

Although many Portuguese speak English, learning a few phrases can make interactions warmer and more rewarding. These were lifesavers during my time in smaller towns:

- Bom dia – Good morning
- Por favor – Please
- Obrigado/Obrigada – Thank you (masculine/feminine)
- Onde fica...? – Where is...?
- A conta, se faz favor** – The bill, please.

At the Instituto Camões Lisbon, located at R. Rodrigues Sampaio 113, 1150-012 Lisbon, I attended a short language workshop. It gave me confidence to navigate conversations at markets and cafés.

12E Address and Location of Popular Accommodations

Finding the right accommodation in Portugal depends on your mood and destination. During a stay in Lisbon, I enjoyed the chic yet cozy LX Boutique Hotel, nestled at Rua do Alecrim 12, 1200-017 Lisbon. Its location, near the Tagus River, makes it perfect for exploring the city's nightlife and cultural spots.

In Porto, I was captivated by The Yeatman, an opulent hotel perched high above the city, offering breathtaking panoramic views of the Douro River. It's perched at Rua do Choupelo 345, 4400-088 Vila Nova de Gaia, an ideal location for wine lovers.

For an authentic experience in the Algarve, I stayed at Casa Mãe, located at Rua do Jogo da Bola 41, 8600-712 Lagos. This boutique hotel blends minimalist design with local craftsmanship, surrounded by the laid-back charm of Lagos.

12F *Address and Location of Popular Restaurants and Cafes*

Food is at the heart of Portuguese culture. In Lisbon, my go-to spot for traditional dishes is Cervejaria Ramiro at Av. Almirante Reis 1, 1150-007 Lisbon. Their garlic-laden shrimp and tender steak sandwiches are unforgettable.

For a more refined experience, I recommend Belcanto, a Michelin-starred restaurant by Chef José Avillez. It's tucked away at Largo de São Carlos 10, 1200-410 Lisbon, offering a modern take on Portuguese cuisine.

While in Porto, I frequently visited Majestic Café, located at Rua Santa Catarina 112, 4000-442 Porto. This historic café, with its opulent interiors and classic pastries, felt like stepping into another era.

12G Address and Location of Popular Bars and Clubs

Lisbon's nightlife is legendary. In Bairro Alto, I stumbled upon Pavilhão Chinês, a quirky bar with walls adorned in eccentric memorabilia. You can find it at Rua Dom Pedro V 89, 1250-093 Lisbon.

For rooftop views and cocktails, I often visited Park Bar, perched atop a parking garage at Calçada do Combro 58, 1200-123 Lisbon. It's a hidden gem with views of the 25th of April Bridge.

In Porto, the liveliness of Galerias de Paris Street is unmatched, with bars like Plano B, located at Rua de Cândido dos Reis 30, 4050-151 Porto, offering music and art under one roof.

12H *Address and Location of Top Attractions*

Portugal's iconic landmarks are spread across its cities and countryside. In Lisbon, no trip is complete without a visit to the Jerónimos Monastery at Praça do1400-206 Lisboa. Its exquisitely detailed Manueline architecture held me utterly mesmerized.

In Sintra, the colorful turrets of Pena Palace at Estrada da Pena, 2710-609 Sintra make it one of the most magical spots I've ever visited.

Heading north to Porto, the Dom Luís I Bridge, located at Av. Gustavo Eiffel, 4000-276 Porto, offers breathtaking views of the Douro River and its surrounding vineyards.

12I *Address and Location of Bookshops*

Portugal is a paradise for book lovers. In Lisbon, I frequented Bertrand Bookstore, officially the oldest operating bookshop in the world. It's located at Rua Garrett 73, 1200-203 Lisbon, in the heart of Chiado.

Another gem is Porto's Livraria Lello, celebrated worldwide as one of the most stunning bookstores ever created. Its Neo-Gothic interiors and sweeping staircase at R. das Carmelitas 144, 4050-161 Porto are captivating.

12J Address and Location of Top Clinics, Hospitals, and Pharmacies

For healthcare needs, Lisbon's CUF Descobertas Hospital, located at Rua Mário Botas 199, 1998-018 Lisbon, offers excellent care with English-speaking staff.

In Porto, I had a positive experience at Hospital da Luz Porto, located at Rua de

São João de Brito 221, 4100-455 Porto. It's a modern facility with a reputation for its efficiency.

For pharmacies, I often visited Farmácia Sá da Bandeira in Porto at Rua de Sá da Bandeira 135, 4000-427 Porto, which is conveniently open late.

12K Address and Location of Popular UNESCO World Heritage Sites

Portugal's UNESCO World Heritage Sites are a testament to its cultural and historical richness. The Tower of Belém in Lisbon, located at Av. Brasília, 1400-038 Lisbon, is a stunning example of Manueline architecture.

Another favorite is the Monastery of Batalha at Largo Infante Dom Henrique, 2440-109 Batalha, a masterpiece commemorating Portugal's victory in the Battle of Aljubarrota.

Lastly, the Alto Douro Wine Region, accessible from Peso da Régua, offers terraced vineyards that produce some of the finest Port wines. Start your journey at Quinta do Vallado, located at Vilarinho dos Freires, 5050-364 Peso da Régua, for a truly immersive experience.

Made in the USA
Coppell, TX
25 April 2025